Easy Cauliflower Cookbook

The Effortless Chef Series

By
Chef Maggie Chow
Copyright © 2015 by Saxonberg Associates
All rights reserved

Published by
BookSumo, a division of Saxonberg Associates
http://www.booksumo.com/

Stay To the End of the Cookbook and Receive....

I really appreciate when people, take the time to read all of my recipes.

So, as a gift for reading this entire cookbook you will receive a **massive collection of special recipes.**

Read to the end of and get my *Easy Specialty Cookbook Box Set for FREE*!

This box set includes the following:

1. ***Easy Sushi Cookbook***
2. ***Easy Dump Dinner Cookbook***
3. ***Easy Beans Cookbook***

Remember this box set is about **EASY** cooking.

In the ***Easy Sushi Cookbook*** you will learn the easiest methods to prepare almost every type of Japanese Sushi i.e. *California Rolls, the Perfect Sushi Rice, Crab Rolls, Osaka Style Sushi*, and so many others.

Then we go on to *Dump Dinners*. Nothing can be easier than a Dump Dinner. In the ***Easy Dump Dinner Cookbook*** we will learn how to master our slow cookers and make some amazingly unique dinners that will take almost **no effort**.

Finally in the ***Easy Beans Cookbook*** we tackle one of my favorite side dishes: Beans. There are so many delicious ways to make Baked Beans and Bean Salads that I had to share them.

So stay till the end and then keep on cooking with my *Easy Specialty Cookbook Box Set*!

About the Author.

Maggie Chow is the author and creator of your favorite *Easy Cookbooks* and *The Effortless Chef Series*. Maggie is a lover of all things related to food. Maggie loves nothing more than finding new recipes, trying them out, and then making them her own, by adding or removing ingredients, tweaking cooking times, and anything to make the recipe not only taste better, but be easier to cook!

For a complete listing of all my books please see my author page.

INTRODUCTION

Welcome to *The Effortless Chef Series*! Thank you for taking the time to download the *Easy Cauliflower Cookbook*. Come take a journey with me into the delights of easy cooking. The point of this cookbook and all my cookbooks is to exemplify the effortless nature of cooking simply.

In this book we focus on Cauliflower. You will find that even though the recipes are simple, the taste of the dishes is quite amazing.

So will you join me in an adventure of simple cooking? If the answer is yes (and I hope it is) please consult the table of contents to find the dishes you are most interested in. Once you are ready jump right in and start cooking.

— Chef Maggie Chow

TABLE OF CONTENTS

STAY TO THE END OF THE COOKBOOK AND RECEIVE..2
About the Author. 5
Introduction..7
Table of Contents 8
Any Issues? Contact Me 11
Legal Notes 12
Common Abbreviations 13
Chapter 1: Easy Cauliflower Recipes ...14
    Maggie's Easy Cauliflower Soup 14
    (Vegetarian Approved) 14
    Flame Broiled Cauliflower 18
    Mashed Cauliflower 21
    Cauliflower and Cheese Bake...........24
    Spicy Cauliflower 27
    Oven Roasted Cauliflower................30

Gobi Aloo 36
(Indian Cauliflower) 36
Paleo Rice 39
Cream of Cauliflower Bake 41
Artisan Cauliflower 44
Creamy Leek Soup 47
Buttery Carrots and Cauliflower 50
Mushroom Monterey Casserole 53
Cauliflower Salad I............................56
Cauliflower Masala 59
(Indian Cauliflower II).....................59
Toasted Indian Peas..........................63
Southern Fried Cauliflower..............65
Cauliflower Salad II 68
Cauliflower Fried Bites 71
Cauliflower Salad III.........................74
Chinese Fried Rice 77
Cauliflower Swiss Bake 80
Maggie's Favorite Cauliflower Casserole..83
Indian Cauliflower III 86

THANKS FOR READING! NOW LET'S TRY SOME **SUSHI** AND **DUMP DINNERS**..... 89

Come On... 91

Let's Be Friends :) 91

Can I Ask A Favour? 92

Interested in Other Easy Cookbooks? . 93

Any Issues? Contact Me

If you find that something important to you is missing from this book please contact me at maggie@booksumo.com.

I will try my best to re-publish a revised copy taking your feedback into consideration and let you know when the book has been revised with you in mind.

:)

— Chef Maggie Chow

LEGAL NOTES

ALL RIGHTS RESERVED. NO PART OF THIS BOOK MAY BE REPRODUCED OR TRANSMITTED IN ANY FORM OR BY ANY MEANS. PHOTOCOPYING, POSTING ONLINE, AND / OR DIGITAL COPYING IS STRICTLY PROHIBITED UNLESS WRITTEN PERMISSION IS GRANTED BY THE BOOK'S PUBLISHING COMPANY. LIMITED USE OF THE BOOK'S TEXT IS PERMITTED FOR USE IN REVIEWS WRITTEN FOR THE PUBLIC AND/OR PUBLIC DOMAIN.

COMMON ABBREVIATIONS

cup(s)	C.
tablespoon	tbsp
teaspoon	tsp
ounce	oz.
pound	lb

*All units used are standard American measurements

Chapter 1: Easy Cauliflower Recipes

Maggie's Easy Cauliflower Soup

(Vegetarian Approved)

Ingredients

- 1 tsp extra-virgin olive oil, or as needed
- 1/2 yellow onion, diced
- 1 leek, diced
- 3 cloves garlic, minced
- 1 head cauliflower, cut into florets
- 1/2 head broccoli, cut into florets
- 3 red potatoes, cut into bite-size pieces
- 1 (32 oz.) carton low-sodium vegetable broth
- water to cover

- 1 tbsp nutritional yeast, or more to taste
- 1/2 tsp ground turmeric
- 1 bay leaf
- salt and ground black pepper to taste
- 1 pinch cayenne pepper, or to taste
- 1 (12 fluid oz.) can fat-free evaporated milk
- 3 tbsps whole wheat flour, or as needed
- 1 tbsp curry powder

Directions

- Stir fry your garlic, leeks, and onions in olive oil, in a large pot, for 6 mins.
- Then add: potatoes, cauliflower, and broccoli.
- Cook everything for 6 more mins.
- Now pour in your broth and increase the heat.

- Add some water as well to submerge all the veggies.
- Season everything with: black pepper, curry, cayenne, turmeric, salt, and bay leaves then place a lid on the pot, ajar, and let the contents simmer for 27 mins.
- Get a bowl, combine: flour, yeast, and milk. Then pour everything into the soup.
- Let the soup simmer for 6 more mins.
- Enjoy.

Amount per serving (12 total)

Timing Information:

Preparation	15 m
Cooking	35 m
Total Time	50 m

Nutritional Information:

Calories	74 kcal
Fat	0.7 g
Carbohydrates	13.5g
Protein	4.6 g
Cholesterol	1 mg
Sodium	< 125 mg

* Percent Daily Values are based on a 2,000 calorie diet.

Flame Broiled Cauliflower

Ingredients

- 2 tbsps minced garlic
- 3 tbsps olive oil
- 1 large head cauliflower, separated into florets
- 1/3 C. grated Parmesan cheese
- salt and black pepper to taste
- 1 tbsp diced fresh parsley

Directions

- Grease a baking dish with oil and set your oven to 450 degrees before doing anything else.
- Get a bowl, toss: cauliflower, garlic, and olive oil. Then place everything in the baking dish.
- Add some pepper and salt to the cauliflower before cooking everything in the oven for 30 mins.

- Now add your parsley and parmesan.
- Finally place the casserole dish under the broiler for 6 mins.
- Enjoy.

Amount per serving (6 total)

Timing Information:

Preparation	15 m
Cooking	25 m
Total Time	40 m

Nutritional Information:

Calories	118 kcal
Fat	8.2 g
Carbohydrates	8.6g
Protein	4.7 g
Cholesterol	4 mg
Sodium	111 mg

* Percent Daily Values are based on a 2,000 calorie diet.

Mashed Cauliflower

Ingredients

- 1 lb cauliflower florets
- 1/4 C. mashed potato flakes
- 1/4 C. low-fat milk
- 2 tbsps margarine
- salt and ground black pepper to taste
- 1/4 C. shredded reduced-fat Cheddar cheese

Directions

- Set your oven to 375 degrees before doing anything else.
- With a steamer insert and 2 inches of boiling water steam your cauliflower for 22 mins then place the florets in a bowl.
- Add the following to the bowl as well: margarine, milk and potato flakes.

- Get a potato masher or a big fork and mash the mix.
- Add your pepper and salt and then place all the contents in a casserole dish and cook everything in the oven for 12 mins.
- Enjoy.

Amount per serving (4 total)

Timing Information:

Preparation	15 m
Cooking	30 m
Total Time	45 m

Nutritional Information:

Calories	105 kcal
Fat	6.1 g
Carbohydrates	9.4g
Protein	4.8 g
Cholesterol	2 mg
Sodium	< 247 mg

* Percent Daily Values are based on a 2,000 calorie diet.

Cauliflower and Cheese Bake

Ingredients

- 1 medium head cauliflower, broken into small florets
- 1/4 C. butter
- 2 tsps all-purpose flour
- 1 C. milk
- salt and pepper to taste
- 1/4 C. fine dry bread crumbs
- 3 egg yolks
- 3 egg whites
- 1 C. shredded Cheddar cheese

Directions

- Set your oven to 400 degrees before doing anything else.
- Boil your florets in 3 inches of water for 10 mins. Then remove all the liquid and place the florets to the side.

- For two mins stir flour in melted butter and continue stirring while adding the milk.
- Get the mixture boiling and remove everything from the heat.
- Add the bread crumbs, egg yolks, florets, beaten egg whites, and cheese.
- Pour everything into a baking dish and cook the contents in the oven for 32 mins.
- Enjoy.

Amount per serving (4 total)

Timing Information:

Preparation	15 m
Cooking	30 m
Total Time	45 m

Nutritional Information:

Calories	382 kcal
Fat	27.9 g
Carbohydrates	15.8g
Protein	18.7 g
Cholesterol	225 mg
Sodium	549 mg

* Percent Daily Values are based on a 2,000 calorie diet.

Spicy Cauliflower

Ingredients

- olive oil cooking spray
- 3/4 C. gluten-free baking flour
- 1 C. water
- 1/2 tsp garlic powder, or to taste
- salt and ground black pepper to taste
- 2 heads cauliflower, cut into bite-size pieces
- 2 tbsps butter
- 1/2 C. hot pepper sauce
- 1 tsp honey

Directions

- Coat a casserole dish with nonstick spray and set your oven to 450 degrees before doing anything else.

- Get a bowl, combine: pepper, flour, salt, garlic powder, and water.
- Once everything is smooth add your florets and coat them evenly with the mix.
- Layer everything in the casserole dish and cook the contents for 27 mins.
- Add your honey and hot sauce to some melted butter and stir the mix until it is smooth.
- Now coat your florets with this buffalo sauce. Then bake everything for 8 more mins.
- Let the florets sit for 7 mins before serving.
- Enjoy.

Amount per serving (4 total)

Timing Information:

Preparation	15 m
Cooking	30 m
Total Time	55 m

Nutritional Information:

Calories	133 kcal
Fat	6.2 g
Carbohydrates	17.5g
Protein	6 g
Cholesterol	15 mg
Sodium	907 mg

* Percent Daily Values are based on a 2,000 calorie diet.

Oven Roasted Cauliflower

Ingredients

- 1 large head cauliflower
- 1/2 C. seasoned bread crumbs
- 2 tbsps grated Parmesan cheese
- 1/4 C. margarine, melted
- 1/8 tsp garlic powder
- 1/8 tsp salt
- 1 pinch red pepper flakes
- 1 pinch dried oregano

Directions

- Set your oven to 375 degrees before doing anything else.
- Rinse your cauliflower with fresh water and submerge the cauliflower head, in water, in a big pot.
- Boil the water and let the cauliflower head cook for 22 mins.

- Get a bowl, combine: melted margarine, parmesan, bread crumbs, oregano, garlic powder, pepper flakes, and salt.
- Get a casserole dish and add your cauliflower to it.
- Coat everything with the margarine mix and cook the contents in the oven for 17 mins.
- Enjoy.

Amount per serving (6 total)

Timing Information:

Preparation	5 m
Cooking	40 m
Total Time	45 m

Nutritional Information:

Calories	149 kcal
Fat	8.7 g
Carbohydrates	14.7g
Protein	5 g
Cholesterol	2 mg
Sodium	< 380 mg

* Percent Daily Values are based on a 2,000 calorie diet.

Rustic Cauliflower

Ingredients

- 1 large head cauliflower, sliced lengthwise through the core into 4 'steaks'
- 1/4 C. olive oil
- 1 tbsp fresh lemon juice
- 2 cloves garlic, minced
- 1 pinch red pepper flakes, or to taste
- salt and ground black pepper to taste

Directions

- Set your oven to 400 degrees before doing anything else.
- Combine in a bowl: black pepper, olive oil, salt, lemon juice, pepper flakes, and garlic.
- Layer your cauliflower in a casserole dish evenly.

- Coat the veggies with half of the wet mix and cook everything in the oven for 17 mins.
- Flip the veggies and coat them with the remaining mixture.
- Continue cooking everything for 14 more mins.
- Enjoy.

Amount per serving (4 total)

Timing Information:

Preparation	10 m
Cooking	30 m
Total Time	40 m

Nutritional Information:

Calories	176 kcal
Fat	13.8 g
Carbohydrates	12.1g
Protein	4.3 g
Cholesterol	0 mg
Sodium	64 mg

* Percent Daily Values are based on a 2,000 calorie diet.

Gobi Aloo

(Indian Cauliflower)

Ingredients

- 1 tbsp vegetable oil
- 1 tsp cumin seeds
- 1 tsp minced garlic
- 1 tsp ginger paste
- 2 medium potatoes, peeled and cubed
- 1/2 tsp ground turmeric
- 1/2 tsp paprika
- 1 tsp ground cumin
- 1/2 tsp garam masala
- salt to taste
- 1 lb cauliflower
- 1 tsp diced fresh cilantro

Directions

- Stir fry the following, in oil: ginger paste, cumin seeds, and garlic for 2 mins.
- Now add your potatoes and the following spices: salt, turmeric, garam masala, paprika, and cumin.
- Place a lid on the pan and let the contents cook for 8 mins while stirring the mix every 2 mins.
- Now add the cilantro and florets.
- Place the lid back on the pan and continue cooking everything on low for 10 more mins.
- Stir the contents occasionally.
- Enjoy.

Amount per serving (4 total)

Timing Information:

Preparation	15 m
Cooking	20 m
Total Time	35 m

Nutritional Information:

Calories	135 kcal
Fat	4 g
Carbohydrates	23.1g
Protein	4 g
Cholesterol	0 mg
Sodium	331 mg

* Percent Daily Values are based on a 2,000 calorie diet.

Paleo Rice

Ingredients

- 1 large head cauliflower, cut into large chunks
- 2 tbsps extra-virgin olive oil
- salt and ground black pepper to taste

Directions

- With a blender or food processor blend your cauliflower into small grains similar in size to rice kernels.
- Now fry this cauliflower, in olive oil, for 7 mins, with a lid, and stir everything with a fork.
- Add salt and pepper to taste then serve.
- Enjoy.

Amount per serving (4 total)

Timing Information:

Preparation	10 m
Cooking	5 m
Total Time	15 m

Nutritional Information:

Calories	113 kcal
Fat	7 g
Carbohydrates	11.1g
Protein	4.2 g
Cholesterol	0 mg
Sodium	160 mg

* Percent Daily Values are based on a 2,000 calorie diet.

Cream of Cauliflower Bake

Ingredients

- 1/2 C. uncooked white rice
- 10 oz. broccoli florets
- 10 oz. cauliflower florets
- 1/2 C. butter
- 1 onion, diced
- 1 lb processed cheese food, cubed
- 1 (10.75 oz.) can condensed cream of chicken soup
- 5 3/8 fluid oz. milk
- 1 1/2 C. crushed buttery round crackers

Directions

- Set your oven to 350 degrees before doing anything else.
- Begin to boil water in a large pot.
- Once everything is boiling pour in your rice.

- Get the water boiling again and the place a lid on the pot.
- Set the heat to a low level and cook the rice for 22 mins with a gentle boil.
- Once the rice is done begin to stir fry your onions in butter for 3 mins then add in your: cooked rice, cauliflower, and broccoli.
- Toss the veggies in the butter and add the milk, soup, and cheese.
- Cook everything until the cheese has melted and pour the contents into a casserole dish.
- Top the casserole with crackers and cook everything in the oven for 32 mins.
- Let the contents sit for 10 mins then serve.
- Enjoy.

Amount per serving (7 total)

Timing Information:

Preparation	40 m
Cooking	30 m
Total Time	1 h 10 m

Nutritional Information:

Calories	545 kcal
Fat	38.8 g
Carbohydrates	30g
Protein	20.5 g
Cholesterol	101 mg
Sodium	1544 mg

* Percent Daily Values are based on a 2,000 calorie diet.

Artisan Cauliflower

Ingredients

- 1 large head cauliflower, cut into florets
- 3 C. chicken broth
- 3 tbsps butter
- 1 C. shredded Vermont white Cheddar cheese
- 1/4 C. grated Parmesan cheese
- salt and pepper to taste

Directions

- Get a large pot and get your broth boiling. Once it is boiling add in your florets and place a lid on the pot.
- Lower the heat and let the contents lightly boil for 12 mins.
- Now remove the lid and continue simmering everything until about

1/2 of the liquid has evaporated (8 to 10 mins).
- Shut the heat and add in: parmesan, cheddar, and butter.
- Mash the contents together with a large fork or masher then add your pepper and salt.
- Enjoy.

Amount per serving (4 total)

Timing Information:

Preparation	10 m
Cooking	25 m
Total Time	35 m

Nutritional Information:

Calories	270 kcal
Fat	20 g
Carbohydrates	11.8g
Protein	13.7 g
Cholesterol	58 mg
Sodium	395 mg

* Percent Daily Values are based on a 2,000 calorie diet.

Creamy Leek Soup

Ingredients

- 2 tbsps olive oil
- 3 tbsps butter
- 3 leeks, cut into 1 inch pieces
- 1 large head cauliflower, diced
- 3 cloves garlic, finely diced
- 8 C. vegetable broth
- salt and freshly ground black pepper to taste
- 1 C. heavy cream (optional)

Directions

- Stir fry your garlic, cauliflower and leeks in butter and olive oil for 12 mins.
- Add the broth and get everything boiling.
- Now place a lid on the pot and set your heat to low and let everything simmer for 50 mins.

- Grab an immersion blender and puree the soup.
- Add your pepper, salt and cream and continue to use the blender.
- Serve the mix once the soup is smooth.
- Enjoy.

Amount per serving (12 total)

Timing Information:

Preparation	15 m
Cooking	1 h
Total Time	1 h 15 m

Nutritional Information:

Calories	155 kcal
Fat	13.1 g
Carbohydrates	8.3g
Protein	2.4 g
Cholesterol	35 mg
Sodium	346 mg

* Percent Daily Values are based on a 2,000 calorie diet.

Buttery Carrots and Cauliflower

Ingredients

- 3/4 C. water
- 1 C. cauliflower, diced
- 1 C. cubed potatoes
- 1/2 C. finely diced celery
- 1/2 C. diced carrots
- 1/4 C. diced onion
- 1/4 C. butter
- 1/4 C. all-purpose flour
- 3 C. milk
- salt and pepper to taste
- 4 oz. shredded Cheddar cheese

Directions

- Boil the following for 12 mins: water, onions, cauliflower, carrots, potatoes, and celery.
- Get a large pot and cook your flour in melted butter for 2 mins

while stirring. Then shut the heat and add in the milk while continuing to stir.
- Turn the heat back on and keep stirring until everything is thick.
- Now add your cauliflower, pepper, and salt.
- Finally stir in your cheese until it is melted and shut the heat.
- Let the soup sit for 10 mins.
- Enjoy.

Amount per serving (4 total)

Timing Information:

Preparation	20 m
Cooking	25 m
Total Time	45 m

Nutritional Information:

Calories	385 kcal
Fat	24.7 g
Carbohydrates	25.9g
Protein	15.7 g
Cholesterol	75 mg
Sodium	368 mg

* Percent Daily Values are based on a 2,000 calorie diet.

Mushroom Monterey Casserole

Ingredients

- 6 slices turkey bacon, or more to taste
- 1 large head cauliflower, cut into florets
- 1/2 C. sour cream
- 1/2 C. mayonnaise
- 1 clove garlic, minced
- 1/2 tsp salt
- 1/4 tsp ground black pepper
- 2 C. shredded Colby-Monterey Jack cheese, divided
- 1 (8 oz.) package baby bella mushrooms, roughly diced
- 6 tbsps diced fresh chives, divided

Directions

- Set your oven to 425 degrees before doing anything else.
- Fry your bacon for 10 mins then remove any excess oils before breaking the bacon into pieces.
- For 20 mins steam your cauliflower using a steamer insert over 2 inches of boiling water.
- Get a bowl, combine: 1 C. Monterey, black pepper, chives, cauliflower, sour cream, mushrooms, salt, bacon, mayo, and garlic.
- Evenly distribute the mix throughout your casserole dish and cook everything in the oven for 22 mins.
- Let the casserole sit for 10 mins before serving.
- Enjoy.

Amount per serving (8 total)

Timing Information:

Preparation	15 m
Cooking	45 m
Total Time	1 h

Nutritional Information:

Calories	346 kcal
Fat	29.3 g
Carbohydrates	9.2g
Protein	14.4 g
Cholesterol	63 mg
Sodium	780 mg

* Percent Daily Values are based on a 2,000 calorie diet.

Cauliflower Salad I

Ingredients

- 1 C. broccoli florets
- 1 C. cauliflower florets
- 2 C. hard-cooked eggs, diced (optional)
- 1 C. shredded Cheddar cheese
- 6 slices bacon
- 1 C. mayonnaise
- 1/2 C. white sugar
- 2 tbsps white wine vinegar

Directions

- Fry your bacon then remove any excess oils and break it into pieces.
- Get a big bowl and layer: cauliflower, bacon, eggs, broccoli, and cheese.
- Get a 2nd bowl, mix: vinegar, mayo, and sugar.

- Pour the wet mix over the layers and chill everything in the fridge for 10 mins before serving.
- Enjoy.

Amount per serving (8 total)

Timing Information:

Preparation	10 m
Cooking	15 m
Total Time	25 m

Nutritional Information:

Calories	400 kcal
Fat	33 g
Carbohydrates	15.5g
Protein	11.2 g
Cholesterol	177 mg
Sodium	453 mg

* Percent Daily Values are based on a 2,000 calorie diet.

Cauliflower Masala

(Indian Cauliflower II)

Ingredients

- 1 (16 oz.) package tofu
- 1/2 C. plain yogurt
- 2 tbsps lemon juice
- 2 tsps ground cumin
- 1/2 tsp cayenne pepper
- 1 tsp paprika
- 1 tsp garam masala
- 1 tbsp minced fresh ginger root
- 2 tbsps unsalted butter
- 4 cloves garlic, minced
- 3 serrano peppers, seeded and minced
- 4 tsps ground coriander
- 2 tsps ground cumin
- 2 tsps garam masala
- 1/2 tsp salt
- 1 (16 oz.) can tomato sauce
- 1 small head cauliflower, cut into florets

- 2 C. half-and-half cream
- 1 C. frozen peas
- 1/4 C. diced fresh cilantro

Directions

- Put your tofu between two plates and place a skillet on top of one plate to apply pressure on the tofu and help it drain.
- Drain the tofu, in this position, for 40 mins.
- Set your oven to 375 degrees before doing anything else.
- Cut your tofu into half an inch cubes.
- Get a bowl, combine: ginger, yogurt, half of your masala, lemon juice, paprika, tofu, cumin, and cayenne.
- Evenly distribute your tofu throughout a cookie sheet and cook them in the oven for 1 hour.
- Turn the tofu pieces every 20 mins.

- Simultaneously stir fry your serrano and garlic in butter for 4 mins than add: cumin (2 tsps), the remaining masala, coriander and salt.
- Cook the mix for one for min then pour in your tomato sauce and cauliflower.
- Place a lid on the pan and let the contents simmer for 17 mins.
- Now add in half and half, peas, tofu, and cilantro.
- Cook the mix for 7 more mins.
- Enjoy over cooked basmati rice.

Amount per serving (4 total)

Timing Information:

Preparation	20 m
Cooking	50 m
Total Time	1 h 30 m

Nutritional Information:

Calories	421 kcal
Fat	27.3 g
Carbohydrates	30g
Protein	20.5 g
Cholesterol	62 mg
Sodium	1038 mg

* Percent Daily Values are based on a 2,000 calorie diet.

Toasted Indian Peas

Ingredients

- 3 tbsps vegetable oil
- 4 tsps cumin seed
- 1 tsp mustard seed
- 2 C. green peas
- 2 C. cauliflower florets
- 1 tsp salt

Directions

- Toast your mustard and cumin seeds in hot oil until they pop and then add in the florets and peas.
- Add some salt and place a lid on the pan.
- Cook the contents for 17 mins with a lower level of heat.
- Enjoy.

Amount per serving (4 total)

Timing Information:

Preparation	10 m
Cooking	20 m
Total Time	30 m

Nutritional Information:

Calories	174 kcal
Fat	11.3 g
Carbohydrates	14.4g
Protein	5.5 g
Cholesterol	0 mg
Sodium	604 mg

* Percent Daily Values are based on a 2,000 calorie diet.

Southern Fried Cauliflower

Ingredients

- 1 head cauliflower, broken into small florets
- 1 egg
- 2 tsps milk
- 1 C. cracker crumbs
- 4 C. oil for deep frying

Directions

- Boil your florets in water and salt for 10 mins. Then remove all the liquid.
- Get a deep fryer or big pan hot with oil to 375 degrees.
- Get a bowl, mix: milk, and eggs.
- Get a 2nd bowl to hold your cracker crumbs.

- Coat the cauliflower with egg, then crumbs, and fry the florets in the hot oil until golden.
- Place them on paper towels to drain.
- Enjoy.

Amount per serving (8 total)

Timing Information:

Preparation	30 m
Cooking	20 m
Total Time	50 m

Nutritional Information:

Calories	270 kcal
Fat	19.6 g
Carbohydrates	20.4g
Protein	3.9 g
Cholesterol	23 mg
Sodium	287 mg

* Percent Daily Values are based on a 2,000 calorie diet.

Cauliflower Salad II

Ingredients

- 1 C. mayonnaise
- 1/4 C. freshly grated Parmesan cheese
- 2 tbsps white sugar
- 1 (10 oz.) package spring lettuce mix
- 1/2 C. freshly grated Parmesan cheese
- 1/2 C. grated carrot
- 1/2 C. small cauliflower florets
- 1/2 C. bacon bits

Directions

- Get a bowl, combine: sugar, mayo, and a quarter C. parmesan.
- Place everything in the fridge for 8 hrs covered in plastic wrap.

- Get a big bowl, toss: bacon bits, lettuce, parmesan, cauliflower, and carrots.
- Coat the veggies with the mayo mix and toss again.
- Enjoy.

Amount per serving (8 total)

Timing Information:

Preparation	
Cooking	15 m
Total Time	12 h 15 m

Nutritional Information:

Calories	285 kcal
Fat	26.1 g
Carbohydrates	6.4g
Protein	7.5 g
Cholesterol	24 mg
Sodium	536 mg

* Percent Daily Values are based on a 2,000 calorie diet.

Cauliflower Fried Bites

Ingredients

- 6 C. cauliflower florets
- 1/2 C. all-purpose flour
- 3 extra large eggs
- 1 tsp baking powder
- 1 (.7 oz.) package dry Italian-style salad dressing mix
- 1/2 C. olive oil for frying, or as needed

Directions

- Blend the cauliflower in a blender until finely done. Then place it in a bowl.
- Add to the cauliflower Italian dressing, flour, baking powder, and eggs.
- Mix the contents evenly.
- Get a frying pan hot with olive oil.

- For 3 mins per side fry a tbsp of cauliflower mix.
- Then flip the fritter and continuing frying it for 3 more mins.
- Continue frying in this manner for all of the mix. Then place the fritters on some paper towel to drain.
- Enjoy.

Amount per serving (6 total)

Timing Information:

Preparation	10 m
Cooking	10 m
Total Time	20 m

Nutritional Information:

Calories	129 kcal
Fat	4.9 g
Carbohydrates	15.3g
Protein	6.7 g
Cholesterol	108 mg
Sodium	682 mg

* Percent Daily Values are based on a 2,000 calorie diet.

Cauliflower Salad III

Ingredients

- 1 head cauliflower, cut into florets
- 1/2 C. grape tomatoes, quartered
- 3 tbsps bacon bits
- 1/4 C. shredded Cheddar cheese
- 3 hard-boiled eggs, diced
- 1 C. mayonnaise
- 1/3 C. sugar
- 2 tbsps vinegar
- 1 tbsp lemon juice

Directions

- Boil some water in a big pot with your eggs.
- Once the water is boiling place a lid on the pot and shut the heat.
- Let the eggs soak in the hot water for 15 mins. Then remove the shells on the eggs and dice them.

- Get a bowl, toss: eggs, florets, cheese, tomatoes, and bacon bits.
- Get a 2nd bowl, mix: lemon, vinegar, mayo, and sugar.
- Combine the mayo mix with the florets and toss everything to evenly coat the veggies.
- Place the salad in the fridge for 10 mins.
- Enjoy.

Amount per serving (6 total)

Timing Information:

Preparation	15 m
Cooking	15 m
Total Time	30 m

Nutritional Information:

Calories	408 kcal
Fat	34.6 g
Carbohydrates	18.5g
Protein	8.4 g
Cholesterol	128 mg
Sodium	415 mg

* Percent Daily Values are based on a 2,000 calorie diet.

Chinese Fried Rice

Ingredients

- 2 C. frozen peas
- 1/2 C. water
- 1/4 C. sesame oil, divided
- 4 C. cubed pork loin
- 6 green onions, sliced
- 1 large carrot, cubed
- 2 cloves garlic, minced
- 20 oz. shredded cauliflower
- 6 tbsps soy sauce
- 2 eggs, beaten

Directions

- Boil your peas in water for 7 mins. Then remove all the liquid.
- Now get a wok and stir fry your pork in sesame oil for 10 mins. Then put it aside.

- Add in the rest of the oil and stir fry: garlic, carrots, and onions for 7 mins.
- Then add in cauliflower and cook the mix for 6 more mins.
- Add the soy sauce and pork and continue stir frying everything for 4 more mins.
- Slide your pork mix over to make some space in your wok and begin to your fry whisked eggs, then scramble the eggs (4 mins) and combine them with the pork.
- Let the rice sit for 10 mins.
- Enjoy.

Amount per serving (6 total)

Timing Information:

Preparation	15 m
Cooking	30 m
Total Time	45 m

Nutritional Information:

Calories	366 kcal
Fat	19.2 g
Carbohydrates	15.8g
Protein	33.3 g
Cholesterol	132 mg
Sodium	1065 mg

* Percent Daily Values are based on a 2,000 calorie diet.

Cauliflower Swiss Bake

Ingredients

- 1 large head cauliflower, cut into florets
- salt and pepper to taste
- 2 medium tomatoes, sliced
- 1/2 C. butter, melted
- 8 oz. Swiss cheese, shredded

Directions

- Set your oven to 350 degrees before doing anything else.
- Microwave your florets for 6 mins submerged in water.
- Remove the liquid and add in pepper and salt.
- Top the florets with the tomato pieces and coat everything with melted butter and cheese.
- Cook the contents in the oven for 43 mins in a casserole dish.

- Enjoy.

Amount per serving (8 total)

Timing Information:

Preparation	10 m
Cooking	45 m
Total Time	55 m

Nutritional Information:

Calories	241 kcal
Fat	19.6 g
Carbohydrates	8.3g
Protein	10.1 g
Cholesterol	57 mg
Sodium	218 mg

* Percent Daily Values are based on a 2,000 calorie diet.

Maggie's Favorite Cauliflower Casserole

Ingredients

- 1 head cauliflower, separated into florets
- 1 C. sour cream
- 1 C. shredded Cheddar cheese
- 1/2 C. crushed corn flakes
- 1/4 C. finely diced green bell pepper
- 1/4 C. finely diced red bell pepper
- 1 tsp salt
- 1/4 C. grated Parmesan cheese
- paprika (optional)

Directions

- Oil a casserole dish and set your oven to 325 degrees before doing anything else.
- With a steamer insert cook your cauliflower for 10 mins over 2

inches of boiling water then set the veggies aside.
- Get a bowl, mix: salt, sour cream, bell peppers, cauliflower florets, corn flakes, and cheddar.
- Pour everything into the casserole dish and cook the contents in the oven for 36 mins.
- Enjoy.

Amount per serving (8 total)

Timing Information:

Preparation	10 m
Cooking	35 m
Total Time	45 m

Nutritional Information:

Calories	169 kcal
Fat	12.6 g
Carbohydrates	7.5g
Protein	7.8 g
Cholesterol	33 mg
Sodium	486 mg

* Percent Daily Values are based on a 2,000 calorie diet.

Indian Cauliflower III

Ingredients

- 1 large head cauliflower, broken into small florets
- 1 (10.75 oz.) can condensed cream of chicken soup
- 3/4 C. mayonnaise
- 1/4 C. milk
- 2 tsps curry powder
- 12 wheat crackers
- 1/4 C. melted butter

Directions

- Coat a baking dish with nonstick spray or oil and set your oven to 350 degrees before doing anything else.
- Steam your cauliflower with a steamer insert over 2 inches of boiling water for 10 to 15 mins.

Then place them in the baking dish.
- Get a bowl and combine: curry, soup, milk, and mayo.
- Get a 2nd bowl, combine: crumbled crackers, and melted butter.
- Coat your cauliflower with the mayo mix and then the melted butter mix.
- Now cook everything in the oven for 35 mins.
- Enjoy.

Amount per serving (8 total)

Timing Information:

Preparation	15 m
Cooking	30 m
Total Time	45 m

Nutritional Information:

Calories	286 kcal
Fat	25.6 g
Carbohydrates	12.5g
Protein	3.9 g
Cholesterol	27 mg
Sodium	478 mg

* Percent Daily Values are based on a 2,000 calorie diet.

Thanks for Reading! Now Let's Try some Sushi and Dump Dinners....

Send the Book!

To grab this **box set** simply follow the link mentioned above, or tap the book cover.

This will take you to a page where you can simply enter your email address and a PDF version of the **box set** will be emailed to you.

I hope you are ready for some serious cooking!

<u>Send the Book!</u>

You will also receive updates about all my new books when they are free.

Also don't forget to like and subscribe on the social networks. I love meeting my readers. Links to all my profiles are below so please click and connect :)

<u>Facebook</u>

<u>Twitter</u>

Come On...
Let's Be Friends :)

I adore my readers and love connecting with them socially. Please follow the links below so we can connect on Facebook, Twitter, and Google+.

Facebook

Twitter

I also have a blog that I regularly update for my readers so check it out below.

My Blog

CAN I ASK A FAVOUR?

If you found this book interesting, or have otherwise found any benefit in it. Then may I ask that you post a review of it on Amazon? Nothing excites me more than new reviews, especially reviews which suggest new topics for writing. I do read all reviews and I always factor feedback into my newer works.

So if you are willing to take ten minutes to write what you sincerely thought about this book then please visit our Amazon page and post your opinions.

Again thank you!

INTERESTED IN OTHER EASY COOKBOOKS?

Everything is easy! Check out my Amazon Author page for more great cookbooks:

For a complete listing of all my books please see my author page.

Printed in Great Britain
by Amazon